The
Little Book
To
Defeat
Depression

Denisia Hockley

PREFACE

We know that the first 4 or so years of life profoundly shape our emotional and relational circuits. The last decade has seen an explosion in the field of developmental neuroscience, its intersections with attachment dynamics, and its impact on how we nurture children (the fundamental starting point of every person). Professionals like Dan Seigal and Allan Schore come to mind. Yet there is another level, we also know intuitively that every 'good enough' mother (to use Winnicott's practical term) somehow manages to come through with the goods, even if she has never read a word of Dan Seigal. The Little Book Series (in particular Your Child the Little Scientist) values developmental science that confirms the nature and shape of "good enough" nurturance BUT deviates from typical ways of teaching so as to avoid getting lost in technical detail. The Amazing Abilities of Your Magical Mind goes even further by taking cutting edge scientific thinking and presenting concepts that are both exciting and challenging to your belief system.

Denisia Hockley

CONTENTS

Denisia Hockley

The Little Book
To
Defeat Depression

Hands up anyone who has NEVER felt depressed!

Depression is something we all experience at some time in our lives!

It is NOT your identity!
It is NOT who you are!
It is NOT permanent!
It does NOT mean you are weak, dumb or crazy!

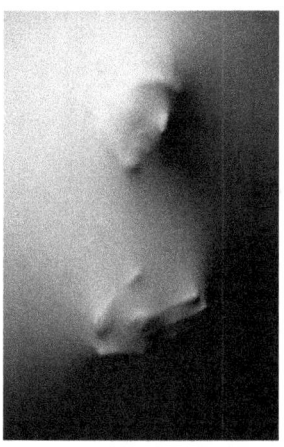

One aspect of your life is not your whole identity…

So you have depression and/or anxiety… !

You have nothing to feel guilty or ashamed about! You do not need to hide your feelings OR pretend everything is OK. (Although we will talk about the benefits of fake-it-till-you-make-it: more on that later).

You are not alone!

In this little book you will find answers, understanding and solutions to those times when life sux and you feel desperate, isolated, helpless and without hope!

Remember too; we ALL get depressed without necessarily 'having' depression.

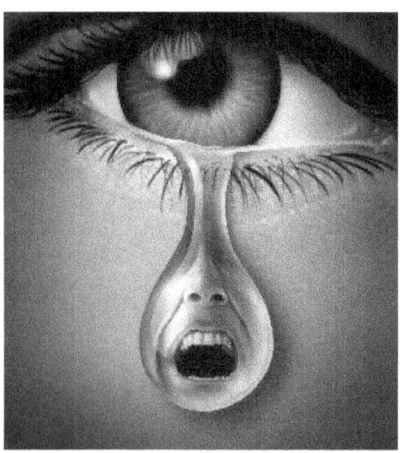

If only other people understood!

It is not their fault and it is not yours! Unfortunately most people do not understand poor mental health unless/until they have experienced it themselves. Even then if they have not had these things explained to them they may project a less than helpful or supportive attitude towards what you are currently going through. You may need to avoid people, around whom you feel worse – at least until you are starting to get on top of this. AND YOU WILL BE!

It seems like no one understands: feeling isolated, misunderstood, like you just want to give up on everything – even your doctor/therapist does not seem to understand that no matter how hard you try to feel better, to get on with your life, to carry out therapy homework, sometimes you just cannot…!!! (Or at least that is how it feels)

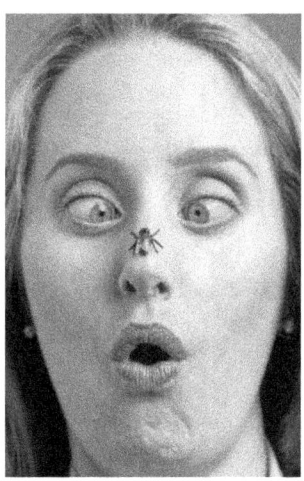

Try not to focus on the small things

If controlling your own mind is hard, changing how you feel can be even more challenging but you can do it!! Yes it can be a daily struggle AND yes there are days when you want to give up!

And NO it is not helpful when 'well-meaning' people tell you to just snap out of it! BUT you are going to have to do a lot of appropriate self-talk to get through this, (No telling yourself "I'm being stupid" is not OK). If you can afford a therapist or you have one solid person with whom you can share anything and everything that's great. But you don't need anyone nagging or criticizing you for being where you are right now! Those clichés like 'there is always someone worse off' or 'it could be worse' or 'count your blessings' are great when you are feeling stronger but right now you need to understand exactly what you are going through and what you can do about it.

Do Not Identify with Depression: It is not who you are!

Achievement, like behavior is not who you are!
Doing one dumb thing doesn't make you dumb!
Failing at something does not make you a failure!
Acting out a bad behavior does not in itself make you (or others) a bad person.

Having depression does not mean you are a negative, angry or miserable person!

Think about it, you may be a person with a disability, a person with lots of money or a large debt, a person with a drinking problem, a person with 2 big toes on one foot... Whatever! You are also many other things.... Like a person with a dog, a person who likes chocolate, who swims, works and does a whole lot of good stuff..

When you feel good tell your friends....

When you feel bad tell your therapist...!

You would not drive your car for years without a checkup and a service; and yet you may be a little reluctant to see a doctor and a psychologist to maintain a healthy body and mind!

AT THE END OF THE DAY THERE ARE ONLY EVER 2 POSSIBLE OUTCOMES: YOU SUCCEED OR YOU GIVE UP!

LET ME REPEAT…. THERE ARE ONLY EVER TWO OUTCOMES – YOU GIVE UP! OR YOU KEEP FIGHTING UNTIL YOU WIN!

Giving up is really not an option now is it!

What is depression?

Types:

Reactive- In simple terms something happens in your life which is more than you can cope with at this time. Perhaps you have been coping with a number of stressors and this event is the last straw. Perhaps you were happy and healthy and now you have fallen in a heap. THIS DEPRESSION/ ANXIETY IS A 'REACTION' 'RESPONSE' TO STRESSFUL EVENT/S. Usually this means that with a little time, support (& medication '**maybe**'), you will gradually get better while you resolve or get used to what has happened.

Pre-dispositional (aka- endogenous) Endogenous tends to imply that it comes from within in you, that you are a depressive or anxious type of person, I prefer to say pre-dispositional; meaning that for whatever reason you are more sensitive or vulnerable to stressful situations. It does not mean that you are destined to be depressed; it does mean that you need to work a little harder, than some other people, at coping with life's ups and downs. You need to be a little kinder and more nurturing toward **yourself**.

You can still learn life/coping skills that will enable you to lead a happy healthy life.

Who gets depressed?

Mental health does not discriminate! It affects the poor and the wealthy! The smart and the not-so-smart! In fact – the more intelligent you are the more vulnerable you may be – that's right? You thought you were stupid because you have not been able to beat this thing? WRONG!

Chances are you spend a lot of time thinking and analyzing situations; it is also likely that you expect a lot of yourself. You are harder on yourself than on others!! AND that you are maybe a little too in touch with reality!

Symptoms:

Be careful when assessing your own symptoms because there can be a number of explanations. A therapist or doctor looks at symptoms in context with a number of other things. Here are some things that MIGHT indicate depression!

Sleep patterns – too much, too little, restless, broken, poor quality…

Eating- too much, too little, comfort eating…

Thoughts – worry, rumination, simple paranoia (NO THAT DOESN'T MEAN YOU ARE PSYCHOTIC), self-defeating, hopelessness, over-reactive, over-sensitive, unusually judgmental, pessimistic, fearful, destructive…

Physical symptoms- stress can cause just about any physical symptom- including nausea, headaches, dizziness, heartburn, back pain or pain anywhere in your body, intestinal disturbances (I.B.S), menstrual problems….BUT always always get any symptoms checked out by your doctor, **do not assume** they are caused by stress.

Lack of motivation and/or energy- Lack of control - feeling you have no control over your responses, your emotions, your body, your life….. You know what you need to do, what you 'should do' AND you really want to, BUT your body and your emotions won't behave in the way you want/ need them to.

HEY IT IS HARD!

Yes you can beat it but it IS hard! Damn Hard!

Now we have acknowledged that it IS hard – we will not focus on negatives and negative language (read Magical Mind for full explanation). The trick is to approach each day separately, that is, each day you try to do the things you need to, if you fail today – LET IT GO and try again tomorrow! And tomorrow, and all the tomorrows until you get there….

NOTE: Some people may not understand why you have 'dropped your bundle' especially if you have always appeared to others as a strong confident person! Before you judge someone's inability to cope, remember, you do not know just how big their bundle became before they dropped it!

Medication

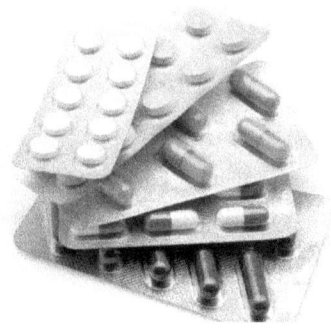

The following is intended to provide a simplistic lay person's understanding of medication used with depression and anxiety symptoms, it is not fully comprehensive and is not intended to replace or contradict formal medical or pharmacological advice.

Types: Generally speaking the types of medication you need to be aware of are: SSRIs (SNRIs): Antidepressants most used today- There are several on the market and essentially they are all as good as each other.

*It is generally really hard for your doctor to predict which will be the best for you. Chances are the first one you try will work for you, however you may have to try several before you and your doctor determine the one that is perfect for you. You may need patience and perseverance to find the right one. A long list of 'possible' side effects includes nausea, head-spins, headaches, dizziness, anxiety – and many more (sometimes it is best not to read the list, especially if you are prone to a bit of paranoia).

Reality is, most people will probably get a little light headed and icky in the tummy! Your sleep may be affected in either direction! This would 'usually' last between 3 days and 2 weeks:

If your side effects are worse/different or last longer go back and talk to your doctor but do not stress. Do not keep taking meds that are not working for you after a reasonable length of time – go talk to your therapist/doctor. Do not hesitate to get more than one opinion. Sorry but doctors and therapist are people and none of us are perfect! The more information you give your doctor the better chance s/he has of choosing an SSRI/SNRI most likely to suit you BUT your bio chemistry is unique to you, and your doctor cannot know for sure which will suit you. The good news is that it is extremely rare for anyone not to suit at least one of the SSRI's and once settled the results can be really good – a client once said "wow, this must be what normal people feel like"

(Be sure to read section on washout and weaning off meds!)

TCAs: Antidepressants used before SSRIs came along-still appropriate for some people/situations today (In many cases I actually prefer clients to use these). Use as prescribed, make sure your doctor explains use and abuse.

Benzodiazepines: you know them as Valium, Serapax, Xanax, Temazapan, Normison (if not sure check the label) – "Supa-glue & Band-aides" they certainly do have their place and they can really help you hold it together in a stressful situation SHORT TERM! But if you over-use them they will not only cease to help you but will have a paradoxical effect – that is, using too many or using them too often can actually make you more depressed/anxious.

NOTE: For many people Xanax can cause psychotic like episodes so be very very careful and NEVER NEVER self-medicate on these little buggers.

* Neuro/Biofeedback technology may soon be able to help us identify the right antidepressant medication for you... (Prof. Leon Petchkovsky, Pinniger Clinic, Robina, Qld. Aust [2009])

Over-use of meds like benzodiazepines will mean that they may not work for you when you really need them. Unfortunately most people build up a tolerance to these meds, meaning that you have to keep taking more to get the same effect then after a while you will not only become dependent but they will start to make you more anxious and depressed. This is one med you really must treat with respect and use sparingly and only as prescribed.

Sleeping pills: Temazapan, Normison, Stillnox & Others; Use only as a last resort and only for very short periods of time. In the long term they will not resolve your sleeping problems (see session on sleep). You may also have problems with bizarre dreams or nightmares as ell as 'day-after' sluggishness and mood issues. These meds also lead to dependence and tolerance effects if over-used. ALSO be wary of over-the counter sleep remedies – many people over-use these medication because they think over-the-counter means take as many as you like – Not So! Based on many patient reports I would stay well away from Stillnox the side effects for MANY people have been horrific!

Natural or Herbal remedies: You must advise your doctor if you are taking these as some will have a bad interaction with your prescription meds. e.g.; St John's Wort must not be taken with SSRI's

Stigma: In a perfect world there would be no stigma attached to taking antidepressant medication (or no such thing as stigma would be cool too); essentially it is your business, if the people around you are judgmental and insensitive – do not tell them (half of them are probably taking them too).

Wash out: If it is necessary for you to change your meds your therapist/ doctor will explain the wash out period, which is different depending on which meds you are changing from/to. And again, people handle wash out differently. During this change-over time (usually only a few days) you need to be prepared for temporary side effects such as nausea, head-spins etc., if you understand that these are normal for wash out you should be able to cope by taking a little extra care of yourself and avoid doing too much during this period. It helps to know why you feel the way you do and that it will soon pass. Wash out is the chemical side of things BUT coming off completely is a whole other story…read on!

Weaning off antidepressant meds: Too often people decide to stop their meds abruptly; because they are finally feeling well, or they just do not want to be dependent on meds any longer. Very few people (if any) can cease antidepressant meds **abruptly** without experiencing some very uncomfortable side effects. IF the time is right to stop your meds AND you have discussed this with your therapist/doctor: REMEMBER the more time you take to wean off your meds the more likely you will be able to stay off them,

Depending on your dosage start by reducing by an eighth or a quarter (or less in some cases) of the dose (you may be able to break/shave your tablet or you may need to get a lower dosage pill prescribed). You MUST discuss this with your doctor! Stay on the reduced dose until you feel as well as you did on the full dose. Gradually reduce meds in this manner – take your time… Do Not Be In a Hurry, it is quite ok to take months to wean off these meds.

NEVER, NEVER, NEVER USE YOUR FRIEND'S MEDS OR SHARE YOUR MEDS WITH A FRIEND – THEY MAY BE PERFECT FOR YOU BUT MAY BE DANGEROUS FOR SOMEONE ELSE

Choosing your doctor…Your doctor should be someone with whom you share mutual respect and trust. You should feel that your doctor listens to you and understands. But hey, your doctor is not psychic, will not remember everything you told him/her last time and probably does have too many patients to remember everything about you. IT IS YOUR RESPONSIBILITY to remind doctor of your allergies, to ask questions, tell him/her if you disagree and/or need clarification. It is perfectly OK to ask for a second opinion! You should not feel intimidated or helpless when communicating with your doctor or therapist.

THE DOCTOR/ THERAPIST /PATIENT RELATIONSHIP SHOULD BE BASED ON MUTUAL GOOD COMMUNICATION, RESPECT AND UNDERSTANDING

Other People

Dealing with other people: People can be cruel, judgmental and insensitive. They may tell you to 'snap out of it' 'stop being negative' they probably mean well, but if it was that simple to 'snap out of depression" I would not be writing this book!

Mostly the people around you feel helpless, they may want to help but simply do not know how. Many people do not know how to 'listen' without feeling a need to 'fix', which of course they cannot.

Some people will end up avoiding you because they do not know what else to do; others may get mad at you for the same reason.

Breathing…Relaxation….Alpha Brain Rhythms (see Magical Mind and Annihilate Anxiety)

C.B.T.

(What is that????)

Simple really;   You think, you feel, you behave!

Much of psychology today is based on the concept that your emotions and behaviors are largely determined by your thoughts!

Your thoughts are essentially based on (interpreted by) past attitudes, beliefs & experiences as well as other stuff on your hard drive. So where did your beliefs etc., come from? (read Little Scientist)

Schemas, blueprints, models; in short – you learned them, they were probably modeled for you by others. And they are all on your hard drive. You probably believe that all your beliefs are the absolute truth! (That isn't very likely now is it?) BUT: You have been basing most of your attitudes, behavior and responses on these programs from your hard drive!

One of your programs (core beliefs) may say that unless you succeed at everything you are a failure! One of your schemas might be that if a person cries they are weak... You may believe that you are silly or stupid because you were told that once (or many times)... So...

You act off these beliefs...

Learning about CBT (Cognitive Behavior Therapy) and how it relates to you will help you…

Recognize the connection between Thoughts, Emotions & Behaviors. Monitor your own negative/automatic thoughts (cognitions)

Identify and alter distorted beliefs and thinking styles which predispose you to distort your (interpretation) experiences.

Substitute irrational beliefs for interpretations/ ideas which are more factual and realistic.

Increase behaviors that work for you instead of against you… AND combat ANXIETY & DEPRESSION!!!!!!!

Learn to listen to your thinking……… change the way you interpret your surroundings and events you are involved in or exposed to…

By changing your interpretation you are in a better space to change your response /reaction….Become aware of your feelings…..ALLOW YOURSELF TO FEEL WHATEVER YOU NEED TO FEEL!

We all know about intellectualizing but you need to emotionalize sometimes! (Especially in therapy) As we grow we develop 'Cognitive Maps,' programs that help us make sense of the world….Stereotypes, Attitudes, Beliefs and Choices (all of these can be positive, negative or neutral) many of them work well for us.

How our core beliefs (cognitive maps) influence our view of the world affects how we interpret events, situations and feedback from people and the environment; and importantly how we respond to events.

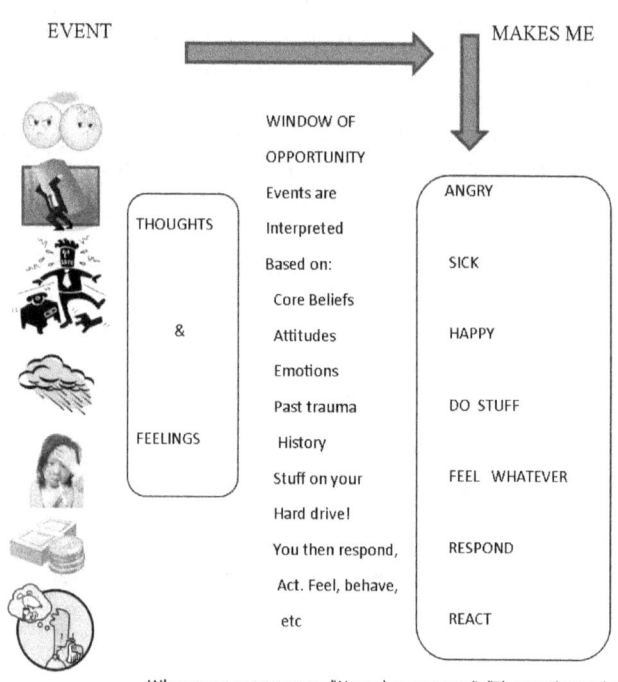

EVENT   MAKES ME

THOUGHTS

&

FEELINGS

WINDOW OF
OPPORTUNITY
Events are
Interpreted
Based on:
Core Beliefs
Attitudes
Emotions
Past trauma
History
Stuff on your
Hard drive!
You then respond,
Act. Feel, behave,
etc

ANGRY

SICK

HAPPY

DO STUFF

FEEL WHATEVER

RESPOND

REACT

Whenever a person says.. "He makes me angry" "The weather makes me blah"

Or any event, situation, memory, behavior etc etc (past or present)" MAKES ME"........

Sorry but that just isn't possible!!!!!!!!!!!!

An EVENT happens OR you remember something: It is then processed through your thoughts and feelings AND based on things like those in the WINDOW OF OPPORTUNITY You respond by getting 'angry' 'sad' 'feeling good' whatever...... GOOD NEWS! This means you have the power to change how you feel, behave and Respond to events in your life!

HOW WE UNDERSTAND CAUSE AND EFFECT i.e.: Because of X and Y it must be Z……but in fact there are many other explanations!!!!!!!!!!! Correct attribution gives us control over our life, that is, our world views are consistent with reality.

HOWEVER if they are incorrect or faulty! We can become socially anxious; i.e. people are laughing at you, talking about you etc etc etc when in fact they are not! SO when you MISS-INTERPRET FEEDBACK from your environment you might become depressed, anxious or unhappy.

Think of this in terms of internal and external locus (location) of control!

Think of personal examples of when you do this?

In general Internal Locus of Control gives you power where external is quite literally out of your control and may make you feel inadequate as though it makes no difference what you do, obviously in terms of the weather and other people's behavior you have little or no control, however you ALWAYS have some control over your responses and choices.

IF YOU HAVE BEEN ABUSED AS A CHILD YOUR PERCEPTIONS OF CONTROL MAY BE SERIOUSLY DAMAGED (Not however, beyond repair) **Read my book 'Your Child the Little Scientist"

Problem Solving:

List all possible solutions no matter how seemingly impossible or improbable. Look at preferred solution/s. List reasons for and against going with each solution. What is needed to carry this out? Assess these possibilities. What will work? What MAY work? What won't work? Be realistic, optimistic and totally honest (No that is not a contradiction).

If a preferred solution doesn't look viable, then look at the next preference. Do the same assessment of how, why and what is needed. Keep going down the list until you find a solution that works for you.

NOTE: It is important that you assess what you can and can't do without being emotional; try to imagine it is someone else's problem and you are helping them with it.

Some situations are genuinely out of your hands....

So MAYBE ALL YOU CAN DO IS TRY TO STAY CALM AND KEEP YOUR HEAD.... FORTUNATELY YOU HAVE **SOME DEGREE** OF CONTROL IN **MOST** SITUATIONS

SUGGESTIONS FOR MOTIVATING YOURSELF

Plan your day (write a list)
☺☺☺☺☺☺☺☺☺☺☺☺☺☺☺☺☺☺☺
☺ It won't happen overnight…but it WILL HAPPEN

Reward yourself for everything you get done. If you set 30 minutes to spend doing something and find it is too long, try for 2 x 15 minutes or 3 x 10. Every little bit helps

Keep reminding yourself of the benefits of small achievements…even if you haven't seen them yet

CHALLENGE thoughts that say "what if" I fail… (Instead think about how you will feel when you succeed)

NEVER AVOID YOUR THERAPIST APPOINTMENT BECAUSE YOU DID NOT ACHIEVE ANY OF YOUR GOALS (HOMEWORK)! IT IS NOT SCHOOL, YOU WON'T GET DETENTION

Getting to Sleep and Staying There

If you have my sleep CD, USE IT! IT WORKS!

It has a buildup effect, so use it regularly (see others in CD-Therapy set)

Try to have a routine where possible

Go to bed when you are sleepy

Do not nap during the day (10 minute power naps are ok if you do not have a sleep problem to begin with) Try and get up the same time each day (even on weekends)

Try to keep bed for sleeping and romance! If possible avoid watching TV and studying in bed. We want your mind to associate bed with a cue to "Go to sleep: Now!"

AVOID CAFFEINE: That's coffee, red bull, coke, etc…It does keep you awake, so work out what time you have to stop having caffeine if you are to sleep that night. Alcohol and drugs make you sleep in the short term, BUT it isn't the right sort of sleep and it MAY make your ongoing sleep problem worse. THE SAME with sleeping pills, they can be a great short-term fix, or a means to catch up on some sleep, but in the LONG-TERM you need some SLEEP SKILLS

Sleep with a friend

Lying in bed WORRYING stimulates your mind and keeps you awake SO if you can't put it out of your mind – write it down to be dealt with tomorrow. Then put something else in your mind – like music, or your sleep CD, or even indulge in a daydream/fantasy (good visualization opportunity)

Use your problem solving techniques before bed time so that you can tell yourself you have a plan to deal with those worries... Obviously if you haven't expended any energy during the day you won't be tired... EXERCISE during the day will help you sleep (it may not happen overnight but it WILL happen)

Eat regularly and avoid large meals before bed time. Carbs give you energy so you need them to start your day. Protein restores and repairs while you sleep. Indigestion OR empty tummy noises will keep you awake... Make sure your bedroom is dark, quiet, and have the TV off. A hot drink (especially MILK) before bed DOES help. Don't put yourself in a position where you are looking at the clock all night, get rid of it or cover it up.

Some lucky people can sleep anywhere....

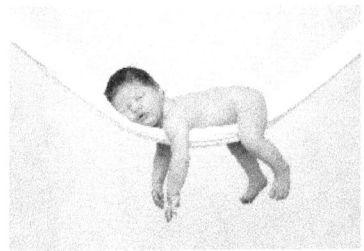

NOTE TO PARENTS:

When you are going off at Miss. 2 yr. old for not going to sleep on demand- ask yourself how easy it is to do that yourself!!!!!

Be Fair!

Learn to relax under any circumstances

Be yourself

Basic Needs of Life

- SUN
- FUN
- MODERATION
- TO DAYDREAM
- GOOD FOOD
- EXERCISE
- AFFECTION
- PHYSICAL SAFETY AND SECURITY
- FINANCIAL SECURITY - ENOUGH TO MANAGE
- FRIENDSHIP
- BEING LISTENED TO
- FEELING HEARD
- GUIDANCE
- RESPECT
- VALIDATION
- EXPRESSING FEELINGS: INCLUDING ANGER
- SENSE OF BELONGING
- NURTURING
- INTIMACY
- SEXUAL EXPRESSION
- LOYALTY AND TRUST
- SENSE OF ACHIEVEMENT
- THE RIGHT TO BE WRONG
- TO FEEL WORTHY
- HOPE
- SENSE OF FREEDOM AND INDEPENDENCE

NOT NECESSARILY IN THIS ORDER

Getting Active

Do something different

Activities consist of…

- Things you NEED to do
- Things you WANT to do
- AND things you can 'get around to' if and when you feel like it…
  WHEN DEPRESSED YOU DON'T FEEL LIKE DOING MUCH SO YOU HAVE TO FORCE YOURSELF TO DO SOME THINGS –

Often you end up feeling a sense of achievement that you actually got SOMETHING done!

EXERCISE: Plan your day/week or if that's TOO hard start with planning the next few hours: (OK so you don't like 'exercise' but I guarantee there are ways of moving your body that you do enjoy…..

That's also called exercise

BREAK IT UP into:

Pleasure activities……(it is essential to incorporate pleasure/leisure/fun activities into everyday)

Daily living requirements……At first this may just be getting up, showering and eating…

Longer term living requirements…eg: paying bills, making phone calls, organizing your life…

SO!!!!!!!!!

Start NOW!

Your first activity is TO   …………..   ????

(Come on you can think of something~)

IF YOU WAIT UNTIL YOU FEEL LIKE DOING IT, IT MAY NOT GET DONE!

So encourage yourself NOW! Even if you do a little bit of something you will start to be proud of yourself and you can build on that….

It is never OK for someone else to nag you!

BUT sometimes it is good to nag yourself!

NEGATIVE   THOUGHTS   ARE   ACTIVITY BLOCKERS……

THOUGHTS SUCH AS..

•NO POINT IN TRYING

•NOT GOOD ENOUGH

•NOT SMART ENOUGH

•PROBABLY FAIL ANYWAY

•ETC ETC ETC

SELF DEFEATING FEELINGS AND THOUGHTS LEAVE YOU DISCOURAGED. FEELING INADEQUATE, HELPLESS, HOPELESS, AND USELESS!!!

This results in disinterest, poor motivations and more depression. Remember, we can do this without meds BUT the option to use anti-depressants is always on the table and there is no shame in getting that extra short term help if you can't push through without it.

Normal Moods: Moods are an important part of our everyday experiences and add color and diversity to our quality of life. From time to time everyone feels "down" or "pissed off" or "flat" or just plain "icky".

Sadness, concern, disappointment and annoyance can be useful emotional responses in situations that didn't turn out the way you wanted. These feelings are often an indication that some effort is required to re-adjust or that something constructive must be done to deal with your feeling or to change the situation. Chose to turn it into an opportunity to grow: Start using your "stress energy" Sometimes even getting mad at a situation can make you get up and fix it!

Keeping a Mood Diary......

When we feel depressed, our view of the world tends to be darker and we are more likely to recall low feelings rather than happy feelings. Sometimes when people are depressed, they find it difficult to recall how they felt on a particular day last week, or last month.

They also find it hard sometimes to gauge whether their mood is improving or not and what events trigger changes in mood. Keeping a mood diary for a few days a week doesn't take much time or effort and it gives insight as to how you've been feeling at different times over the previous week. Detailed notes may even alert you to things that trigger low moods. A mood diary will also assist in measuring changes in your feelings over a longer period of time, perhaps weeks or months. This gives us an idea of whether your depression is lessening as well as what patterns surround or predict episodes.

Three times a day, take a couple of minutes to rate your mood and anxiety level. Try to keep it to the same time e.g. after breakfast, before lunch etc.

If there has been something significant about your day, write it down (note all the good stuff and the not-so-good events). If you miss a time or miss a whole day – don't stress, just continue with the next rating time.

The most important part of this activity is to keep a record of how you feel at any given time.

Is your view of the world limited?

AT THE END OF THE DAY MAKE CHOICES YOU CAN LIVE WITH.

It is ok to be wrong!!!!!

It is ok NOT to be perfect!!!!

It is ok to be AVERAGE!!!

ESSENTIAL FACTORS OF COPING:

ACCEPT THAT THERE IS A PROBLEM/ISSUE WHATEVER YOU WANT TO CALL IT: DENIAL IS SOMETIMES OK, BUT ONLY FOR A VERY LITTLE TIME AND ONLY TO GIVE YOU TIME TO CATCH YOUR BREATH; IT POSTPONES ACTION, IT DOES NOT REPLACE IT.

Get information: Knowledge and Insight are powerful tools to help you understand yourself, others and life. KNOWLEDGE IS POWER

SELF-EMPOWERMENT PROMOTES SELF ESTEEM, RELIEVES ANXIETY & COMBATS DEPRESSION:

COPING WITH SETBACKS

Occasional setbacks are inevitable in life. We can predict that you may experience a bit of a relapse when your life involves significant changes e.g. moving house, changing jobs, getting married (it doesn't have to be something bad to cause you stress). At such times, negative thoughts and feelings may take hold and you think you are back where you started. It is what it is; a bump in the road; a little slip; pick yourself up, shake yourself off and get back in the ring!

Even if you do slip backwards, you will not go all the way. You have not failed! If you allow yourself to think you have failed you may trigger more negative thoughts.

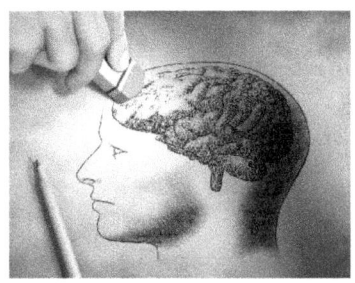

REMOVING PROBLEMS FROM YOUR LIFE WOULD BE A QUICK FIX BUT LEARNING HOW TO RESPOND DIFFERENTLY WILL SERVE YOU FOREVER

Remember the road to recovery is rarely smooth. With the right attitude and good planning you will soon feel better and be able to tackle the things you used to do before the setback. When you do hit a bump, try to identify what has led to the setback and attempt to solve it while at the same time learning more about yourself and the situation. Re-read these books to remind yourself of all the things you have learned. GIVE YOURSELF CREDIT FOR EVERYTHING YOU HAVE LEARNED POSITIVE REINFORCEMENT WORKS WONDERS!

(Remember: If right now you are way too low to even read or comprehend anything, you need antidepressants to help you get to a place where you are able to work on yourself)

Make sure that you attribute your setback to correct causes. Don't blame yourself for something that you couldn't help or foresee; something that you had no control over. Illness and accidents can happen to anyone, no-one can definitively foresee the future. On the other hand claim responsibility for making yourself feel better as quickly as possible. Better still, use the setback as a new opportunity for learning and watch yourself emerge as a stronger more confident and more effective personality.

Laughter is so important no matter 'who' you are!

Protective Factors

Protect yourself from getting depressed:

Be nice to YOU

Allow yourself to be YOU

Do not compare yourself with others (you do not really know their stuff anyway)

Allow yourself to make mistakes (just like the rest of us)

Build up your self-esteem (if others won't tell you how good you are TELL YOURSELF)

Everyone has some good qualities (even if they are hard to find)

Express your feelings and thoughts ASSERTIVELY & APPROPRIATELY

Establish social supports; this can be a tough one, but what do you have to lose? There are so many other people out there JUST LIKE YOU, ask for help in finding them!

Reduce unnecessary stress by planning, time management and being realistic about what you can reasonably do (Today! In the short term! In the long term!)

DO WHAT YOU CAN PLUS A TINY BIT MORE!

Express yourself

Eat good food!

Cuddle someone you love

Hang out with good friends

Or enjoy some alone time

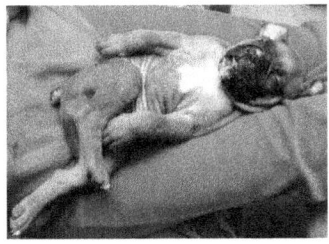

Runaway thoughts

Some dynamics of depressive thinking: Albert Ellis' A B C (short version)

(See 'Makes Me' chart)

A Activating Event

The activating event can be anything – something that happens to us, something that somebody says or does, even something internal – an idea or memory that is triggered.

B Beliefs & Thoughts

Can be beliefs or attitudes such as: A real man must be able to provide for his family: Or they can be visual images like an image of your father standing over you,

Or perhaps brief automatic thoughts such as "I'm a FAILURE". This also includes the constant chatter of self-talk that goes on in our head

C Consequence

This includes anything that follows as a consequence of A-B, For example: feelings, behaviors, sensations, other thoughts include depression, anxiety, and anger and avoidance behavior.

START CHALLENGING YOUR THOUGHTS TODAY!!!!!!! Where is the evidence????

Errors of logic, or cognitive distortions/non-productive thinking styles, are quite common in everyday thinking we all do it; it's just worse when you're depressed...

Read through the following examples of non-productive thinking/cognitive distortions/errors in logic and think about personal examples of each (we all have them from time to time we just need to be aware and edit them when they happen).

**Overgeneralization refers to drawing global conclusions about worth, ability or performance on the basis of a single fact. Consider a person who fails to fix a leaky tap in the house. Many people would call a plumber and then forget about it. But the depressed person may overgeneralize and start to believe they are a useless person, who is unable to fix ANYTHING,

**Magnification and Minimization are gross errors of evaluation in which small bad events are magnified and large good events are minimized. The inability to find the right color shirt is considered a disaster, but a large pay raise and praise from work is considered trivial.

**Personalization (something we all do) refers to incorrectly taking responsibility for bad events. A neighbor slips on a puddle of water outside the depressed person's house and falls, the person blames themselves for not anticipating and preventing the accident.

**Arbitrary Inference: (jumping to conclusions). You make a negative interpretation even though there are no definite facts to support your conclusion, e.g. Fortune telling:. Predicting the future; mind-reading, concluding people are thinking this or that about you……

Now look at the next list and try writing some of yours down…

Selective Abstraction: (mental filters). You pick out a single negative detail and dwell on it so that your vision of reality becomes distorted

Personal Example:

Overgeneralization: You see a single event as a never ending pattern of defeat.

Personal Example:

Magnification, Catastrophizing, or Minimizing: You exaggerate the importance of mistakes or diminish the value of your achievements.

Personal Example:

Personalization: You see yourself as the cause for negative events which you were not responsible for.

Personal Example:

All or Nothing Thinking: (Black & White/ Dichotomous Thinking). You see things in black and white categories, e.g. If your performance falls short of perfect you see yourself as a failure. There is no middle ground. Beware of words such as always, never, everyone, no-one, everything, and nothing.

Personal Example:

Emotional Reasoning: You assume your negative emotions are actual facts

Personal Example:

Should Statements: (Using ultimatums). These statements reflect the need to be right all the time, never making a mistake, the need to be perfect. The consequence of these thoughts is that you develop guilt when you fall short of your standard, and anger/frustration at not achieving at your expected level.

Personal Example:

Concentrating on weaknesses and forgetting strengths: You only focus on your weaknesses, giving an unbalanced view of yourself. Strengths are seen as unimportant, or not considered at all.

Personal Example:

Using double standards: You expect of yourself what you would not expect of others.

Personal Example:

Exaggerating the Importance of events: You don't stop and ask yourself, "What difference will it make in a week or in 10 years? Will I feel the same way?"

Personal Example:

Taking a pessimistic view of your ability to change a situation: You give up trying because you don't think you can change the situation (can lead to depression, helplessness, and lowered self-esteem).

Personal Example:

Blaming the Past: You blame the events of yesterday/year for how you are today, without taking responsibility for changing yourself and/or your present/future

REMEMBER BLAME IS A CANCER THAT SERVES NO ONE, NOT THE BLAMER NOR THE BLAMEE: INSTEAD FOCUS ON RESPONSIBILITY! (BLAME'S HEALTHY COUSIN) WITH RESPONSIBILITY AND OWNERSHIP COMES THE POWER TO CHANGE AND EXERCISE CONTROL.

Other people's beliefs are not necessarily right, or right for you. Recognize that many of your thoughts are not facts. They are merely assumptions, which influence how you feel and what you do.

Before you can experience any event, you must process it with your mind and give it meaning. You must understand what is happening to you before you can feel it. Therefore it is not the actual events that cause you distress, but your perceptions that result in changes in mood. So when you are depressed or anxious, your thinking may be illogical, unrealistic and irrational. When you are depressed next time try to identify the thought that you are entertaining.

What are the advantages and disadvantages of this way of thinking?

Basics

Sometimes people are ambivalent about challenging certain beliefs, particularly perfectionism.

There is a belief or thought that you have that causes you problems or distress, but it is one that you believe you have to live by, or you think you have to accept it because it was taught to you – then ask yourself: - Am I happy with things the way they are?

-	Are my thoughts/beliefs helping me to achieve what I want out of life?

-	Are my thoughts/beliefs helping me get along with others whom I care about?

-	Is my thinking helping me to feel good about myself and my life?

-	Do the advantages of thinking this way outweigh the disadvantages?

When you identify your own beliefs either by working alone or with a group; or just writing them down; try to rewrite the belief and make it more rational and less problematic.

e.g. Core belief – I have to be liked by everybody or I am worthless!

Rational response – I would like to be liked by everybody but sometimes this is not possible and my worth should not depend on it.

The core belief in this example would result in a lot of distress whereas the rational response would be more conducive to liking yourself, achieving your goals and getting on better with other people. If a lot of your irrational thoughts are similar it may mean that there is a common core belief responsible for these irrational thoughts.

Once you have done this ask yourself how your behavior and feelings will change with your new rational response compared to believing in your core irrational beliefs.

IF YOU DO WHAT YOU HAVE ALWAYS DONE YOU WILL GET WHAT YOU HAVE ALWAYS GOT.

•Examine the evidence

•Find alternative explanations

•De-catastrophize

•Examine the advantages and disadvantages of   different thinking styles

•Rational responses

•Writing your journal

Basic Rights:

•I have the right to ask for what I want.

•I have the right to say no to requests or demands I can't meet.

•I have the right to express all of my feelings, positive or negative.

•I have the right to change my mind.

•I have the right to make mistakes and not need to be perfect.

•I have the right to follow my own values and standards.

•I have the right to say no to anything when I feel I am not ready, it is unsafe, or it violates my values. (or cos I just don't wanna!)

•I have the right to determine my own priorities.

•I have the right not to be responsible for others' behavior, actions, feelings, or problems.

•I have the right to be angry at someone I love.

•I have the right to be uniquely myself.

•I have the right to feel scared and say "I'm afraid".

•I have the right to say "I don't know".

•I have the right not to give excuses or reasons for my behavior.

•I have the right to make decisions based on my feelings.

•I have the right to my own needs for personal space and time.

•I have the right to be playful and frivolous.

•I have the right to be healthier than those around me.

•I have the right to be in a non-abusive environment.

•I have the right to make friends and be comfortable around people.

•I have the right to change and grow.

•I have the right to have my needs and wants respected by others.

•I have the right to be treated with dignity and respect.

•I have the right to be happy.

Basic Myths:

•I must be loved and approved of by all the important people in my life.

•To be worthwhile I must always cope with everything and always be successful. I must be completely, perfectly competent, make no mistakes and achieve in every possible way, if I am to be considered worthwhile.

•Being successful means being the best.

•People who act unfairly or badly (even myself) should be blamed or punished.

•If things don't turn out the way I want them to, then it's a total disaster and unbearable.

•Happiness and my own bad feelings are caused by external factors that are outside of my control. Little can be done about them.

•If something is (or may be) dangerous or frightening, then I should be extremely concerned about it and keep dwelling on it.

•It's easier to avoid and put off something difficult or unpleasant than to face certain problems in life.

•I should be dependent on others and need someone stronger than myself to rely on.

•My problem(s) were caused by event(s) in my past therefore I cannot solve my problem(s) now

•I should be upset by other people's problems and difficulties.

Basic Truths:

It's good to get support from others when I want it but the only person I really need to rely on is me.

My problem(s) may have started in some past event but what keeps it (them) going now are my thoughts and actions and they are under my control.

It is sad to see other people in trouble but I don't help them by making myself miserable.

I can cope with feeling sad and sometimes I can take constructive steps to help.

At the end of the day; the choices may not be great BUT I always have choice!

Emotional Thinking – I feel, therefore I am

Believing that because you feel a certain way then things must automatically be that way. For example, if you feel ugly then it is because you are ugly, or if you feel that you can't cope then it's because you really can't cope or aren't coping. The mistake here is that emotions have no validity by themselves. They are usually the consequences of our own thinking (which often does not reflect accurately the way things are) and you can change them. Feelings, irrespective of how real they are to you, are not objective facts. e.g. "I feel fat in these jeans, I must be fat"

Jumping to Negative Conclusions

Drawing negative conclusions from a situation with no evidence to support it, when there may be conflicting evidence which you ignore. This type of thinking leads to negative, self-critical interpretation which upsets you. e.g. Assuming someone is behaving a certain way without checking for evidence. Assuming people are looking down on you or rejecting you; You know what people are thinking; Expecting the worst to happen without good reason.

SOLUTION - Gathering objective evidence, more than 1 or 2 pieces of information

Consider alternative reasons which may cause someone to act a certain way AND Discussing concerns with others – impartial to situation

Try to see things from a different perspective

Myke Ashley Cooper: Cartoon used with the permission and generosity of the author.

Hopelessness & Worthlessness

Cognitive features of depression:

Specific cognitive aspects appear to be instrumental in maintaining depression. These aspects can be best explained as the cognitive threesome.

A negative conception of the self,

A negative interpretation of life experiences, and

A nihilistic view of the future.

Negative thoughts about self, consist of the depressed person's beliefs that they are a defective, worthless, inadequate failure. Low self-esteem comes from these beliefs. When things go wrong people attribute them to personal unworthiness and failure. Believing they are defective they tend to believe they will never be happy.

The depressed person's negative thoughts about experiences consist of their interpretation that what happened to them is bad. They misinterpret small obstacles as impassable barriers. Even when there are more plausible positive views of their experience, they are drawn to the most negative possible interpretation of what has happened.

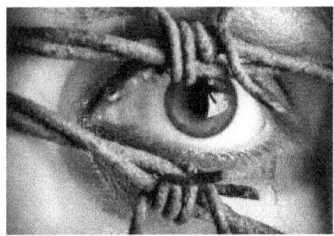

The depressed person's negative view of the future is one of hopelessness. When they think of the future they believe that the negative things that are happening now will continue unabated because of their own personal deficits.

DEPRESSION IS USUALLY TIME LIMITED IT DOES END EVENTUALLY!

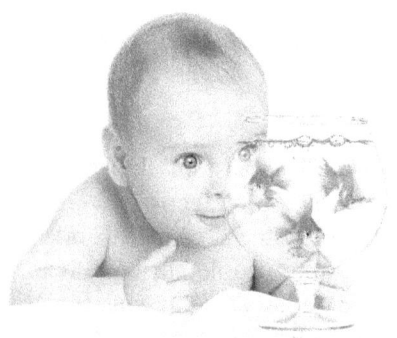

Maintain a child-like curiosity.... Never stop investigating new things!

Some negative thoughts (That we all use at sometimes) Block us from doing the things we want or need to.... Thoughts like.....

•NO POINT IN TRYING

•IT'S USELESS

•I'M HOPELESS

•I'M A FAILURE

Self-defeating ideas and feelings discourage you and make you feel inadequate.

Not trying results in more disinterest, more depression and more feeling of failure.

(See Little Book to Annihilate Anxiety)

We avoid asking someone out on a date by saying to ourselves....things like 'look at what happened last time', now even the thought of asking someone out sends us into a freak out. The problem with avoiding things is that the relief that avoidance may bring is only temporary. In practice, the things we avoid become harder and harder to do and gradually we avoid more and more things.

When we avoid distress provoking situations we do less. Because we generally like consistency in our world (the reason we develop schemas/ blueprints to help us predict and see our world as constant and manageable), we feel more comfortable if our behaviors and our thoughts match. So if we've stopped doing something we tend to change our thoughts and our self-concept to portray ourselves as someone who doesn't do that behavior.

Unfortunately, this can lead to lowered self-esteem and lowered mood and we interpret ambiguous, even positive, feedback from our world in a negative way, confirming our own lowered view of our self. This of course is not pleasant and so our mood lowers further. We tend to become lethargic (we don't want to do things) and apathetic (we don't care if we do or don't do things!) so we find ourselves doing even less. The less we do the less positive reinforcement we receive from our world and so the less incentive we have to do things.

We do less, have a poorer view of ourselves and interpret our world more and more negatively to conform to our negative view; and so it goes on. (Feeding off itself)

OK, so as we can see, avoidance of an anxiety (fear) provoking situation can lead to depression and some very unpleasant and depression-encouraging/ maintaining consequences.

Then what is the cure? If avoiding things you fear makes them harder to face, what would happen if you started to confront your fears? If the fear is reinforced by leaving the situation, what would happen if you stayed put?

Actually if you confronted, for long enough, the thing you fear it would decrease. Most people don't like to put this to the test, so they keep avoiding those situations.

One good way to break the avoidance cycle is to start with easy situations and slowly build up enough confidence to face the harder things. The other important strategy is to control the level of the physical anxiety (fear) using the breathing exercise and staying in the situation until you have become calmer.

But how do you organize such experiences?

First, you make a list of all the situations you avoid. Make sure that you include things that might not be obvious at first, such as certain topics of conversations, missed opportunities, not accepting invitations, putting things off, and cutting activities short. Next, you rank those situations in terms of your need to avoid them, that is, from those situations in which you get anxious but never avoid, to those situations that you always avoid. Then, work your way up the hierarchy (which is the name for the list that you have constructed), confronting your fears at each level until they lose their power to evoke fear.

Exercise: Planning your program of exposure draw up a list of goals that you would like to be able to achieve.

These should be specific goals that vary from being mildly to extremely difficult.

For example;

> To be able to have friends over or dinner
> To be able to go out to a restaurant with friends
> To be able to accept a new job offer

If something is too hard, try to break it down into easier steps to enable   you to work up to the goal a little at a time.

Many fears/anxieties need to be confronted frequently (i.e. 3 or 4 times a week) at first; otherwise your anxiety will rise again by the time you repeat the process. Once you have largely overcome the fear, you may not need to do it as often. The general rule is; the more anxious about something, the more frequently you need to confront it.

Carefully monitor your progress. Keep a diary of your goals, steps, and achievements, together with comments about how you felt and how you dealt with particular situations. This will help you to both structure your progress and give you feedback as to how you are doing. It will also provide you with the opportunity to collect information about how you have tackled situations, which will no doubt be of help in the future.

Practicing the Steps:

If possible use the relaxation exercise before you undertake the activity. Get yourself as calm as possible. (CD). Perform all activities in a slow and relaxed manner. This means giving yourself plenty of time.

Mentally rehearse your activity. For example, if you will be talking with someone, practice what you will say to them. (Visualization) see CD-Therapy

When the circumstances allow, stop your activity at the point which you become anxious. Find a place to sit down, rest and wait for the fear to pass, IT WILL!. If circumstances prevent you from stopping an activity then let yourself continue with no pressure to perform. For example, if there are silences in a conversation let them happen. It is not your responsibility to fill every gap. Do not leave the situation until you feel yourself to be calming down.

Never leave a situation out of fear – face it, accept it, let it fade away, and then either move on or return. If you do not do this, you may see it as a failure and lose confidence.

Congratulate yourself for successful achievements. Do not beat yourself up if you're not quite so successful.

Feeling down causes loneliness and being lonely can bring you down

Feeling depressed can in itself be a cause of loneliness. When people feel depressed, they place less importance on their health, their grooming and appearance. They lose interest in things and often believe that they have nothing to offer. This can lead to withdrawing from social contact or relationships because of the fear of being hurt or rejected. They assume that others see them as dull and uninteresting. Unfortunately, withdrawing from social contact gives more opportunity for brooding and self-pity and will make you even more depressed.

Get a friend to talk to

Demonstrate confidence (fake it till   you make it)

Life can change in a day;

You are never as alone as you may think –

At the end of the day you only have 2 choices,,,

Give up OR Keep going till you win!

Giving Up was never really a choice though was it!

"The Little Book & CD" series.

 Your Child the Little Scientist

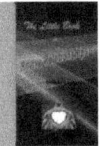 The Little Book to Revive Relationships

 The Little Book to Annihilate Anxiety

 The Little Book to Push Through Pain

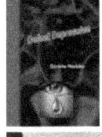 The Little Book to Defeat Depression

 The Little Book to Salvage Self Esteem

 The Little Book to be Physically Phabulous

 Amazing Abilities of your Magical Mind

CD therapy

Anxiety   Alcohol

 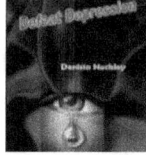

Drugs   Depression

Smoking   Self Esteem

Relationships Pain

Abandonment   Sleep

Anger   Health

 Magical Mind

THE AUTHOR

Denisia Hockley
Clinical Psychologist/Psychotherapist/Author
Dip.Psy.,BA.,BSc.(Hon)Masters Mental Health (Psychotherapy)
Registered AHPRA: (Australia): MAPS Clinical College (Australia)
Member APS (American Pain Society)
Member Association of Independent Authors USA
www.littlebookseries.us
littlebooks2013@gmail.com

Denisia J. Hockley is an Australian Clinical Psychologist: Since 1998 she has worked with everything from general anxiety and depression to victims of trauma and abuse to everyday families struggling with typical life issues as well as those with clinical psychiatric disorders. In 2010 she worked in California specializing in clients with chronic pain issues. As a therapist, she has worked in outback aboriginal settlements, men's correctional facilities, addictions programs and private practice/s. Her style is laidback informal, and solution-focused. As well as CBT, Psycho-education and other general practices she is a qualified psychotherapist and also works with Prof. Leon Petchkovsky with his Neuro feedback clinic. An ex-policewoman, she has had a colorful and diverse career. Denisia's specialties include Complex Post Traumatic Stress Disorder (CPTSD) & Developmental Trauma (non-organic) in adults and adolescents: which result in anxieties, depression, personality disorders, relationship and self-concept difficulties as well as many physiological symptoms including pain and gastrointestinal disorders.

She is most passionate and fascinated by brain science and as she terms it.. The Amazing Abilities of our Magical Minds, She has written a number of book including *Your Child the Little Scientist:* Her Little Book Series address every aspect of life, health, happiness, and mental wellbeing and can be obtained as E-Books at www.littlebookseries.us She also has a series of CD therapies covering Sleep/Addiction/Health & Weight/Anxiety/Depression and more: Visit her site for more information on these.

Bibliography

Albert Ellis   (1995)Clinical Applications of Rational-Emotive Therapy

Albert Ellis   (1995)   Handbook of Cognitive Therapy Techniques

Elizabeth Hills (2006) Getting in touch with your inner bitch,

Jon Kabat-Zinn, (2008)Full Catastrophe Living

MacKay & Fanning (2002) Self Esteem

Manual J Smith (2000) When I say No I feel Guilty

Michael   J Free   (1999) Cognitive therapy in groups: Guidelines and resources in practice

Rudolph Dreikurs (1985) Happy Children

Illustrations & Photography (2012)

Amanda Hockley. Family & Friends

.Istockphotos.com:Fotolia,Dollar photos

Myke Ashley Cooper: Cartoon used with the permission and generosity of the author.